TOOLS OF THE TRADE

SandCastle
Tools of the Trade

WRENCHES

ANDERS HANSON

Consulting Editor, Diane Craig, M.A./Reading Specialist

ABDO
Publishing Company

Published by ABDO Publishing Company, 8000 West 78th Street, Edina, Minnesota 55439.

Copyright © 2010 by Abdo Consulting Group, Inc. International copyrights reserved in all countries.

No part of this book may be reproduced in any form without written permission from the publisher.
SandCastle™ is a trademark and logo of ABDO Publishing Company.

Printed in the United States.

Editor: Pam Price
Content Developer: Nancy Tuminelly
Cover and Interior Design and Production: Mighty Media
Photo Credits: Shutterstock, JupiterImages Corporation

Library of Congress Cataloging-in-Publication Data
Hanson, Anders, 1980-
  Wrenches / Anders Hanson.
     p. cm. -- (Tools of the trade)
  ISBN 978-1-60453-586-0
  1. Wrenches--Juvenile literature. I. Title.

  TJ1201.W8H35 2009
  621.9'72--dc22

                            2008055054

SandCastle™ Level: Fluent

SandCastle™ books are created by a team of professional educators, reading specialists, and content developers around five essential components—phonemic awareness, phonics, vocabulary, text comprehension, and fluency—to assist young readers as they develop reading skills and strategies and increase their general knowledge. All books are written, reviewed, and leveled for guided reading, early reading intervention, and Accelerated Reader® programs for use in shared, guided, and independent reading and writing activities to support a balanced approach to literacy instruction. The SandCastle™ series has four levels that correspond to early literacy development. The levels are provided to help teachers and parents select appropriate books for young readers.

Emerging Readers	**Beginning Readers**	**Transitional Readers**	**Fluent Readers**
(no flags)	(1 flag)	(2 flags)	(3 flags)

SandCastle™ would like to hear from you. Please send us your comments and suggestions.

CONTENTS

combination wrench

WHAT IS A WRENCH?

A wrench is a tool that makes it easier to turn nuts, bolts, and pipes. One end of the wrench grips the object that needs to be turned. A person holds the other end in hand and turns it around the object.

HISTORY

Solymon Merrick **patented** the first wrench in 1835. About 30 years later, J.J. Richardson invented the **socket** wrench.

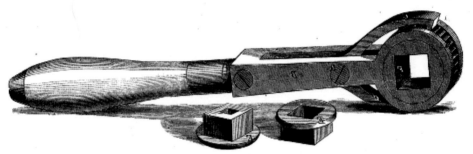

J. J. Richardson's socket wrench

Unlike most wrenches, socket wrenches do not have to be removed and refitted after each turn. The sockets on Richardson's wrench had square openings because nuts and bolts used to be square.

pipe wrench

In 1870, Daniel C. Stillson invented the pipe wrench. He wanted a wrench that could grip and turn metal pipes.

COMBINATION WRENCH

Combination wrenches have two kinds of grips. One grip is in the shape of a circle. This is a box-end grip. The other grip is shaped like the letter *C*. It's called an open-end grip.

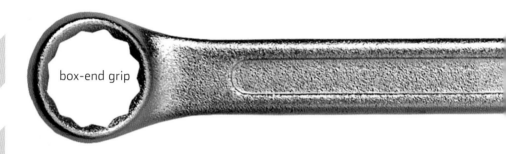

box-end grip

The bolt head fits snugly inside this open-end grip.

This box-end grip is too large for the nut inside it.

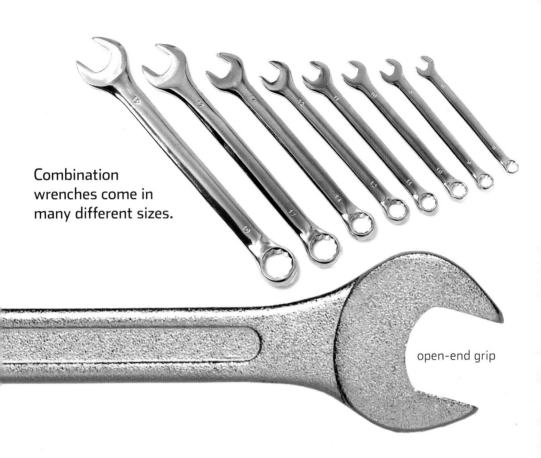

Combination wrenches come in many different sizes.

open-end grip

Both ends fit the same size nut or bolt.

Jimmy uses a combination wrench
to tighten bolts on machines.

Don turns a nut with a combination wrench.
He is fixing a bicycle.

ADJUSTABLE WRENCH

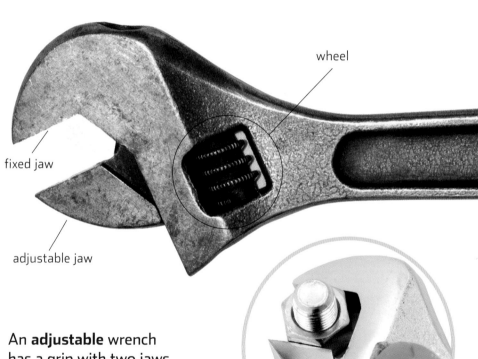

wheel

fixed jaw

adjustable jaw

An **adjustable** wrench has a grip with two jaws. Turning the wheel moves the adjustable jaw up or down.

Close the jaws tightly around an object before turning the wrench.

An **adjustable** wrench can be made to fit different sizes of nuts and bolts.

Ed uses an **adjustable** wrench to tighten bolts. He is repairing a car engine.

Ethan turns a nut with an **adjustable** wrench.
He is fixing his faucet.

PIPE WRENCH

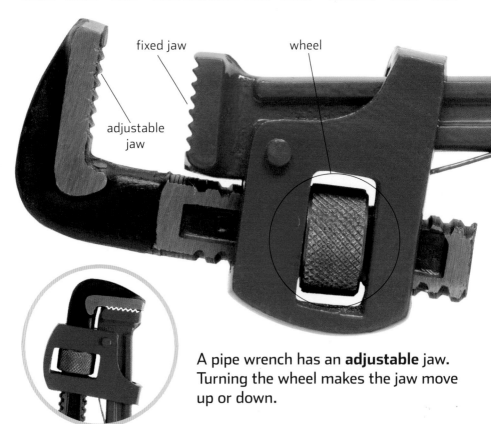

fixed jaw

wheel

adjustable jaw

A pipe wrench has an **adjustable** jaw. Turning the wheel makes the jaw move up or down.

pipe fittings

Plumbers often use pipe wrenches to tighten or loosen **pipe fittings**.

Pipe wrenches grip and turn round objects.

The jaws of a pipe wrench have teeth. The teeth can dig into the object being gripped. This helps the wrench turn smooth, round objects, such as pipes.

Thomas is a **pipe fitter**.
He uses a pipe wrench to cut a pipe.

Jarod's drain pipe is leaky.
He uses a pipe wrench to tighten it.

SOCKET WRENCH

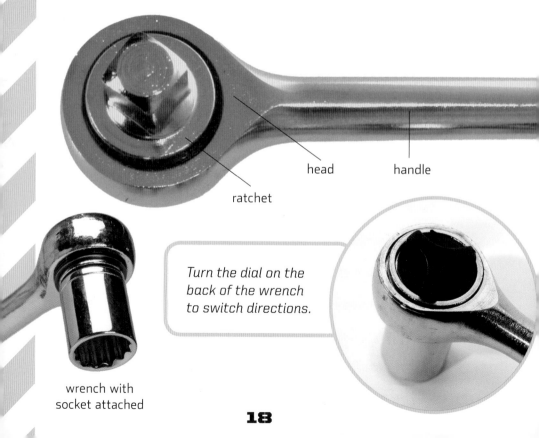

head

handle

ratchet

Turn the dial on the back of the wrench to switch directions.

wrench with socket attached

different-sized sockets

socket wrench set

A **socket** wrench has a handle and removable sockets.

One end of the handle has a **ratchet**. The ratchet controls which direction the socket turns. It can be set to either tighten or loosen.

Allen uses a **socket** wrench to tighten nuts.
He's repairing a car engine.

John tightens a bolt with a **socket** wrench. He is preparing his home for very bad weather.

MATCH GAME

Match the words to the pictures! The answers are on the bottom of the page.

1. socket wrench

A.

2. pipe wrench

B.

3. combination wrench

C.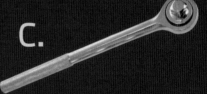

4. adjustable wrench

D.

TOOL QUIZ

Test your tool knowledge with this quiz!
The answers are on the bottom of the page.

1. A combination wrench has one kind of grip. True or false?

2. Adjustable wrenches fit only one size of nut. True or false?

3. Pipe wrenches are useful for turning round objects. True or false?

4. The sockets cannot be removed from a socket wrench. True or false?

Answers: 1) false 2) false 3) true 4) false

GLOSSARY

adjustable – able to be changed slightly.

patent – to obtain an official document giving one person the right to make, use, or sell an invention.

pipe fitter – a person who installs and repairs plumbing.

pipe fitting – an object that connects pipes.

ratchet – a device that allows motion in one direction only.

socket – an opening that holds something, such as a light socket.